Pancake

By James Kaleda

ISBN: 978-0-6151-5652-1

Table of Contents

Introduction

This book was written with the idea that because breakfast is the most important meal of the day, there should be as many recipes as possible for it. We hope you enjoy.

Yield: All recipes are designed to yield approximately sixteen four-inch pancakes.

A note on flour: Since, due to natural sifting, the weight of a dry one cup measure of flour may differ from chef to chef, do not be concerned if you must add slightly more or less flour to achieve the desired consistency.

A note on alcohol: Some of the recipes call for various liquors and spirits. Far be it from the author to recommend consumption of alcohol for breakfast; rest assured the alcohol will evaporate and the concentrated flavor remain.

Ingredients: All ingredients are listed in order of use.

Mixing: Traditionally quick breads call for the mixing of wet and dry ingredients in separate bowls and then combining the two for the final batter. I have not found this useful in the making of pancakes for anything other than the making of an additional dish. I find the most effective way for me is to combine the ingredients in a pitcher, this makes pouring the pancakes all the easier. While you can not over-mix pancakes, it is desirable to have lumps in the batter.

Consistency: The consistency of batter is a matter of personal preference. Thicker batters will yield thicker, denser pancakes and thinner batters will yield thinner, lighter pancakes. If you should find the consistency of my batters either too thick or too thin, I invite you adjust the water to suit your tastes.

Preparing ahead of time: Batters, with the exception of those requiring the separation of eggs, can be prepared up to 24 hours ahead of time. Some additional water and mixing may be required.

About the Author

In 1982 at the age of 6 James Kaleda had his first experience with culinary education. Much to his delight (after being assured that it was ok for boys to cook) his mother enrolled him in "Chemistry in the Kitchen". During this course James and the other young epicureans prepared a variety of recipes and wrote them down. The writing took much longer than the recipe creation.

Two years later, during an attempt to recreate a pretzel recipe learned during "Chemistry in the Kitchen", James did something that would become something of a trade mark. It would follow him through his culinary education and in to his career. It was on that day for the first time that James *set the kitchen on fire.*

Losing his first recipe collection in the fire did not diminish James' youthful love of cooking, although it did cause his *mom* to keep him out of the kitchen for the next several years. Eventually James made his way back into the kitchen at his home and, due to a lack of available ingredients and the twelve mile walk to the local grocery store, began experimenting with substitutions. He completed his culinary education at Warren County Vocational Technical School in 1994 graduating with the Best of Food Service Award.

Since that time James has held many culinary positions but his first love still remains experimenting with flavor combinations - the result of which, in part, is this book.

Pancake Varieties

Basic Pancakes

2 eggs

2 cups milk

¼ cup vegetable oil

2 cups all-purpose flour

2 tablespoons dark brown sugar

2 teaspoons baking powder

1 teaspoon baking soda

1. Heat griddle to 400 degrees (medium high heat)
2. In a large bowl combine eggs, milk, and oil
3. Add flour, sugar, baking powder and baking soda and mix until just combined
4. Pour batter about ¼ cup at a time
5. Cook until edges dry and bubbles form
6. Flip cake and finish cooking, about 15 to 30 seconds

Buttermilk Pancakes

2 eggs

2 cups buttermilk

¼ cup vegetable oil

1¾ cups all-purpose flour

2 tablespoons dark brown sugar

2 teaspoons baking powder

1 teaspoon baking soda

1. Heat griddle to 400 degrees (medium high heat)
2. In a large bowl combine eggs, milk, and oil
3. Add flour, sugar, baking powder and baking soda and mix until just combined
4. Pour batter about ¼ cup at a time
5. Cook until edges dry and bubbles form
6. Flip cake and finish cooking, about 15 to 30 seconds.

Vermont Pancakes

2 eggs

2 cups milk

¼ cup vegetable oil

1½ cups all-purpose flour

½ cup buckwheat flour

2 tablespoons dark brown sugar

2 teaspoons baking powder

1 teaspoon baking soda

1. Heat griddle to 400 degrees (medium high heat)
2. In a large bowl combine eggs, milk, and oil
3. Add flour, sugar, baking powder and baking soda and mix until just combined
4. Pour batter about ¼ cup at a time
5. Cook until edges dry and bubbles form
6. Flip cake and finish cooking, about 15 to 30 seconds

Sourdough Pancakes

2 eggs

2 cups milk

¼ cup vegetable oil

1½ cups all-purpose flour

½ cup sour dough starter*

2 tablespoons dark brown sugar

2 teaspoons baking powder

1 teaspoon baking soda

1. Heat griddle to 400 degrees (medium high heat)
2. In a large bowl combine eggs, milk, and oil
3. Add flour, sugar, baking powder and baking soda and mix until just combined
4. Add starter and mix until incorporated
5. Pour batter about ¼ cup at a time
6. Cook until edges dry and bubbles form
7. Flip cake and finish cooking, about 15 to 30 seconds

For sour dough starter combine 1 cup flour ½ cup water and ¼ tsp active dry yeast cover with plastic wrap and set at room temperature overnight.

Tip: You can use your own sourdough starter if you have one handy. Since the consistency of the starter will vary, it may be necessary to add additional water or flour to reach the desired batter consistency.

Johnny Cakes

2 eggs

2 cups milk

¼ cup vegetable oil

1 cup all-purpose flour

1 cup cornmeal

2 tablespoons sugar

2 teaspoons baking powder

1 teaspoon baking soda

1. Heat Griddle to 400 degrees (medium high heat)
2. In a large bowl combine eggs, milk, and oil
3. Add flour, cornmeal, sugar, baking powder and baking soda and mix until just combined
4. Pour batter about ¼ cup at a time
5. Cook until edges dry and bubbles form
6. Flip cake and finish cooking, about 15 to 30 seconds

Oatmeal Pancakes

2 eggs

2 cups milk

¼ cup vegetable oil

2 tablespoons honey

½ oz Scotch whiskey

1 cup all-purpose flour

1 cup instant oatmeal

2 teaspoons baking powder

1 teaspoon baking soda

1. Heat Griddle to 400 degrees (medium high heat)
2. In a large bowl combine eggs, milk, oil, honey and scotch.
3. Add flour, oatmeal, sugar, baking powder and baking soda and mix until just combined
4. Pour batter about ¼ cup at a time.
5. Cook until edges dry and bubbles form.
6. Flip cake and finish cooking, about 15 to 30 seconds.

Beer Pancakes

2 eggs

12 oz of your favorite beer

¼ cup vegetable oil

1¾ cups all-purpose flour

2 tablespoons dark brown sugar

2 teaspoons baking powder

1 teaspoon baking soda

1. Heat Griddle to 400 degrees (medium high heat)
2. In a large bowl combine eggs, beer, and oil
3. Add flour, sugar, baking powder and baking soda and mix until just combined
4. Pour batter about ¼ cup at a time
5. Cook until edges dry and bubbles form
6. Flip cake and finish cooking, about 15 to 30 seconds

International Pancakes

Crepes

(French Pancakes)

Since there is no leavening agent, these pancakes will be completely flat. They can be served like traditional pancakes or filled with fruit or cheese filling (page 57) then topped with whipped cream.

2 eggs

2 cups milk

¼ cup vegetable oil

2 cups all-purpose flour

2 tablespoons sugar

1. Heat Griddle to 400 degrees (medium high heat)
2. In a large bowl combine eggs, milk, and oil
3. Add flour and sugar and mix until just combined
4. Pour batter about ¼ cup at a time
5. Cook until edges dry
6. Flip cake and finish cooking, about 5 to 15 seconds

***Note** it is not always necessary to flip crepes. In fact some prefer to only cook them on one side.*

Crespelle
(*Italian Pancakes*)
These Italian crepe-like pancakes are traditionally used in savory preparations

6 eggs

2 cups milk

¼ cup vegetable oil

2 cups all-purpose flour

1. Heat Griddle to 400 degrees (medium high heat)
2. In a large bowl combine eggs, milk, and oil
3. Add flour and mix until just combined
4. Pour batter about ¼ cup at a time
5. Cook until edges dry and bubbles form
6. Flip cake and finish cooking, about 15 to 30 seconds

Serving Suggestions: *Serve crespelle filled with cooked spinach and Swiss cheese or cooked chicken and Provolone.*

Pfannkuchen

(*German Pancakes*)

This German pancake is traditionally topped with lemon juice and cinnamon sugar.

6 eggs

2 cups milk

¼ cup vegetable oil

2 cups all-purpose flour

4 tablespoons dark brown sugar

1. Heat griddle to 400 degrees (medium high heat)
2. In a large bowl combine eggs, milk, and oil
3. Add flour and sugar and mix until just combined
4. Pour batter about ¼ cup at a time
5. Cook until edges dry and brown
6. Flip cake and finish cooking, about 10 to 15 seconds
7. Top with cinnamon sugar, juice of one lemon, and fruit jam

Palatschinken
(Austrian Pancakes)

3 eggs

2 cups milk

¼ cup vegetable oil

2 cups all-purpose flour

2 tablespoons dark brown sugar

1. Heat griddle to 400 degrees (medium high heat)
2. In a large bowl combine eggs, milk, and oil
3. Add flour and sugar and mix until just combined
4. Pour batter about ¼ cup at a time
5. Cook until edges dry and brown
6. Flip cake and finish cooking, about 10 to 15 seconds

Blintz
(Russian Pancake)

8 eggs

2 cups milk

2 cups all-purpose flour

1. Heat griddle to 400 degrees (medium high heat)
2. In a large bowl combine eggs and milk
3. Add flour
4. Pour batter about ¼ cup at a time
5. Cook until edges dry and brown
6. Flip cake and finish cooking, about 15 to 30 seconds
7. Fill with cheese (page 57), fruit or potato

Fruit Enriched Pancakes

Caramelized Banana Pancakes

2 eggs

2 cups milk

¼ cup vegetable oil

1 oz rum (optional)

2 cups all-purpose flour

2 tablespoons dark brown sugar

2 teaspoons baking powder

1 teaspoon baking soda

¾ cup diced bananas

½ cup sugar

1. Heat griddle to 400 degrees (medium high heat)
2. In a large bowl combine eggs, milk, rum, and oil
3. Add flour, sugar, baking powder and baking soda and mix until just combined
4. Set batter aside
5. Coat banana pieces in sugar
6. Drop 1 tablespoon of banana for each pancake on the griddle (space far enough apart for pancakes)
7. Grill banana until sugar begins to brown
8. Pour batter about ¼ cup at a time over grilled bananas
9. Cook until edges dry and bubbles form
10. Flip cake and finish cooking, about 15 to 30 seconds

Serve with Caramel Sauce (page 54), or Chocolate Sauce (page 53) or your favorite topping

Pomegranate Honey

2 eggs

2 cups pomegranate juice

¼ cup vegetable oil

4 tablespoons honey

2 cups all-purpose flour

2 teaspoons baking powder

1 teaspoon baking soda

1. Heat griddle to 400 degrees (medium high heat)
2. In a large bowl combine eggs, juice, honey and oil
3. Add flour, baking powder and baking soda and mix until just combined
4. Pour batter about ¼ cup at a time
5. Cook until edges dry and bubbles form
6. Flip cake and finish cooking, about 15 to 30 seconds

Serve with Honey Syrup (page 55), or your favorite topping

Kiwi Raspberry

2 eggs

2 cups cold raspberry tea brewed double strength

1 kiwi peeled and mashed

¼ cup vegetable oil

2 cups all-purpose flour

2 tablespoons sugar

2 teaspoons baking powder

1 teaspoon baking soda

1. Heat Griddle to 400 degrees (medium high heat)
2. In a large bowl combine eggs, tea, kiwi and oil
3. Add flour, sugar, baking powder and baking soda and mix until just combined
4. Pour batter about ¼ cup at a time
5. Cook until edges dry and bubbles form
6. Flip cake and finish cooking, about 15 to 30 seconds

Serve with Honey Syrup (page 55) or your favorite topping

Orange Ginger Pancakes

2 eggs separated

2 tablespoons sugar

2 cups orange juice

¼ cup vegetable oil

2 cups all-purpose flour

2 tablespoons sugar

2 teaspoons baking powder

1 teaspoon baking soda

2/3 cup diced crystallized ginger

1. Heat Griddle to 375 degrees (med heat)
2. Combine egg whites and sugar in a mixing bowl and beat until stiff peaks form, set aside.
3. In a separate bowl combine egg yolks, OJ, and oil
4. Add flour, baking powder and baking soda to yolk mixture
5. Gently fold egg whites into batter
6. Pour batter about ¼ cup at a time
7. Cook until edges dry (bubbles will not form)
8. Flip cake and finish cooking, about 20 to 35 seconds

Serve with Honey Syrup (page 55) or your favorite topping

Pumpkin Pie Pancakes

2 eggs

1½ cups milk

¼ cup vegetable oil

½ cup canned pumpkin

1 teaspoon ground cinnamon

¼ teaspoon ground ginger

¼ teaspoon ground allspice

¼ teaspoon freshly grated nutmeg

1½ cups all-purpose flour

2 tablespoons dark brown sugar

2 teaspoons baking powder

1 teaspoon baking soda

1. Heat griddle to 400 degrees (medium high heat)
2. In a large bowl combine eggs, milk, pumpkin, spices and oil
3. Add flour, sugar, baking powder and baking soda and mix, until just combined
4. Pour batter about ¼ cup at a time
5. Cook until edges dry and bubbles form
6. Flip cake and finish cooking, about 15 to 30 seconds

Variation: for Wicked Pumpkin Pancakes substitute milk for 12 oz of "Pete's Wicked Ale®"

Serve with Caramel Sauce (page 54), or your favorite topping

Strawberry Orange

2 eggs

2 cups orange juice

¼ cup vegetable oil

2 cups all-purpose flour

2 tablespoons sugar

2 teaspoons baking powder

1 teaspoon baking soda

1 cup diced strawberries

1. Heat griddle to 400 degrees (medium high heat)
2. In a large bowl combine eggs, juice, and oil
3. Add flour, sugar, baking powder and baking soda and mix until just combined
4. After batter completely mixed add strawberries
5. Pour batter about ¼ cup at a time
6. Cook until edges dry and bubbles form
7. Flip cake and finish cooking, about 15 to 30 seconds

Cranberry Orange

2 eggs separated

2 tablespoons sugar

1cup cranberry juice cocktail

1 cup orange juice

¼ cup vegetable oil

2 cups all-purpose flour

2 tablespoons sugar

2 teaspoons baking powder

1 teaspoon baking soda

1. Heat Griddle to 400 degrees (medium high heat)
2. In a large bowl combine egg whites and sugar and beat until stiff peaks form
3. In a separate bowl combine egg yolks, juice, and oil
4. Add flour, sugar, baking powder and baking soda to yolk mixture
5. Gently fold egg whites into yolk mixture
6. Pour batter about ¼ cup at a time
7. Cook until edges dry
8. Flip cake and finish cooking, about 15 to 30 seconds

Chocolate Enrichments

Chocolate & Orange Pancakes.........*29*

Chocolate and Strawberries.........*30*

Mocha Latte Pancakes.........*31*

Chocolate Raspberry Pancakes with Caramel Sauce......*32*

Merlot Pancakes with Chocolate sauce.........*33*

Coconut Pancakes with Chocolate Sauce.........*34*

Chocolate Chip Mint.........*35*

Mocha Peach.........*36*

Mexican Chocolate.........*37*

Chocolate & Orange Pancakes

2 eggs

1 cup orange juice

2 oz dark chocolate melted

¼ cup vegetable oil

1¾ cups all-purpose flour

2 tablespoons dark brown sugar

2 teaspoons baking powder

1 teaspoon baking soda

½ cup candied orange pieces (optional)

1. Heat griddle to 400 degrees (medium high heat)
2. In a large bowl combine eggs, juice, chocolate and oil
3. Add flour, sugar, baking powder and baking soda and mix, until just combined
4. Add orange pieces
5. Pour batter about ¼ cup at a time
6. Cook until edges dry and bubbles form
7. Flip cake and finish cooking, about 15 to 30 seconds

Serve with Caramel Sauce (page 54), or Chocolate Sauce (page 53), or your favorite topping

Chocolate and Strawberries

2 eggs

2 cups chocolate milk

¼ cup vegetable oil

2 cups all-purpose flour

2 tablespoons sugar

2 teaspoons baking powder

1 teaspoon baking soda

1 cup diced strawberries

1. Heat griddle to 400 degrees (medium high heat)
2. In a large bowl combine eggs, milk, and oil
3. Add flour, sugar, baking powder and baking soda and mix, until just combined
4. Once batter is completely mixed add strawberries
5. Pour batter about ¼ cup at a time
6. Cook until edges dry and bubbles form
7. Flip cake and finish cooking, about 15 to 30 seconds

Serve with Caramel Sauce (page 54), or Chocolate Sauce (page 53) or your favorite topping

Mocha Latte Pancakes

2 eggs

2 cups espresso or strong coffee

2 oz melted chocolate

¼ cup heavy cream

2 cups all-purpose flour

¼ cup sugar

2 teaspoons baking powder

1 teaspoon baking soda

1. Heat griddle to 400 degrees (medium high heat)
2. In a large bowl combine eggs, espresso, chocolate, and cream
3. In separate bowl combine flour, sugar, baking powder and baking soda
4. Mix dry and wet ingredients together
5. Pour batter about ¼ cup at a time
6. Cook until edges dry and bubbles form
7. Flip cake and finish cooking, about 15 to 30 seconds

Serve with Caramel Sauce (page 54), or Chocolate Sauce (page 53) or your favorite topping

Chocolate Raspberry Pancakes with Caramel Sauce

2 eggs

1 cup milk

2 oz dark chocolate melted

¼ cup vegetable oil

1¾ cups all-purpose flour

¼ cup sugar

2 teaspoons baking powder

1 teaspoon baking soda

2 cups fresh raspberries

Whipped Cream for topping

1. Heat griddle to 400 degrees (medium high heat)
2. In a large bowl combine eggs, milk, chocolate, and oil
3. In separate bowl combine flour, sugar, baking powder and baking soda
4. Mix dry and wet ingredients together
5. Add raspberries
6. Pour batter about ¼ cup at a time
7. Cook until edges dry and bubbles form
8. Flip cake and finish cooking, about 15 to 30 seconds
9. Top with raspberries, whipped cream, and Caramel Sauce (page 54)

Merlot Pancakes with Chocolate sauce

2 eggs

1½ cups merlot

2 oz baker's chocolate melted

1/8 cup vegetable oil

1¾ cups all-purpose flour

1/3 cup sugar

2 teaspoons baking powder

1 teaspoon baking soda

1. Heat griddle to 400 degrees (medium high heat)
2. In a large bowl combine eggs, wine, chocolate and oil
3. Add flour, sugar, baking powder and baking soda and mix until just combined
4. Pour batter about ¼ cup at a time
5. Cook until edges dry and bubbles form
6. Flip cake and finish cooking, about 15 to 30 seconds
7. Top with Chocolate Sauce (page 53)

Coconut Pancakes with Chocolate Sauce

2 eggs

1 cup milk

1 cup coconut milk

¼ cup vegetable oil

2 cups all-purpose flour

2 tablespoons dark brown sugar

2 teaspoons baking powder

1 teaspoon baking soda

½ cup sweetened shredded coconut, toasted

1. Heat griddle to 400 degrees (medium high heat)
2. In a large bowl combine eggs, milk, and oil
3. Add flour, sugar, baking powder and baking soda and mix, until just combined
4. When batter is completely mixed add coconut
5. Pour batter about ¼ cup at a time
6. Cook until edges dry and bubbles form
7. Flip cake and finish cooking, about 15 to 30 seconds
8. Serve with chocolate sauce (page 53)

Chocolate Chip Mint

2 eggs

1¾ cup double strength mint tea

¼ cup vegetable oil

1¾ cups all-purpose flour

2 tablespoons sugar

2 teaspoons baking powder

1 teaspoon baking soda

½ cup mini chocolate chips

1. Heat griddle to 400 degrees (medium high heat)
2. In a large bowl combine eggs, tea, and oil
3. In separate bowl flour, sugar, baking powder and baking soda
4. Mix dry and wet ingredients together
5. Add chocolate chips
6. Pour batter about ¼ cup at a time
7. Cook until edges dry and bubbles form
8. Flip cake and finish cooking, about 15 to 30 seconds

Serve with Chocolate Sauce (page 53) or your favorite topping

Mocha Peach Pancakes

2 eggs

1 cup milk

¾ cup espresso

2 oz dark chocolate melted

¼ cup vegetable oil

1¾ cups all-purpose flour

2 tablespoons dark brown sugar

2 teaspoons baking powder

1 teaspoon baking soda

1 cup diced cooked peaches

1. Heat griddle to 400 degrees (medium high heat)
2. In a large bowl combine eggs, milk, espresso, chocolate, and oil
3. In separate bowl combine flour, sugar, baking powder and baking soda
4. Mix dry and wet ingredients together
5. Add peaches.
6. Pour batter about ¼ cup at a time.
7. Cook until edges dry and bubbles form.
8. Flip cake and finish cooking, about 15 to 30 seconds.

Serve with Caramel Sauce (page 54), or Chocolate Sauce (page 53) or your favorite topping

Mexican Chocolate

2 eggs

1¾ cup milk

2 oz dark chocolate melted

¼ cup vegetable oil

1¾ cups all-purpose flour

¼ tsp grated cinnamon

1/8 tsp chili powder

1 tablespoon dark brown sugar

2 teaspoons baking powder

1 teaspoon baking soda

1. Heat griddle to 400 degrees (medium high heat)
2. In a large bowl combine eggs, milk, chocolate, and oil
3. In separate bowl flour, cinnamon, chili powder, sugar, baking powder and baking soda
4. Mix dry and wet ingredients together
5. Pour batter about ¼ cup at a time
6. Cook until edges dry and bubbles form
7. Flip cake and finish cooking, about 15 to 30 seconds

Other Enrichments

Green Tea Pancakes with Honey Syrup.........*39*

Cheesecake Pancakes.........*40*

Peanut Butter Pancakes.........*41*

Chai Pancakes.........*42*

Espresso and Cinnamon Pancakes with Caramel Cream
Sauce *43*

Parisian Pancakes (Cognac & Kahlua) *44*

Maple Almond Pancakes.........*45*

Honey Almond.........*46*

Green Tea Pancakes with Honey syrup

2 eggs

2 cups double strength green tea

¼ cup vegetable oil

2 cups all-purpose flour

2 tablespoons honey

2 teaspoons baking powder

1 teaspoon baking soda

1. Heat griddle to 400 degrees (medium high heat)
2. In a large bowl combine eggs, tea, oil, and honey
3. Add flour, sugar, baking powder and baking soda and mix until just combined
4. Pour batter about ¼ cup at a time
5. Cook until edges dry and bubbles form
6. Flip cake and finish cooking, about 15 to 30 seconds

Serve with Honey Syrup

Cheesecake pancakes

2 eggs separated

2 tablespoons sugar

4 oz cream cheese softened

4 tablespoons sugar

1¾ cups milk

¼ cup vegetable oil

1¾ cups all-purpose flour

2 teaspoons baking powder

1 teaspoon baking soda

1. Heat griddle to 375 degrees (med heat)
2. In a large bowl combine egg whites and sugar and beat until stiff peaks form
3. In a separate bowl combine, egg yolks, cream cheese, remaining sugar, milk, and oil. Beat until smooth.
4. Add flour, baking powder, and baking soda
5. Gently fold in egg whites
6. Pour batter about ¼ cup at a time
7. Cook until edges dry
8. Flip cake and finish cooking, about 15 to 30 seconds

Serve with Caramel Sauce (page 54), or Chocolate Sauce (page 53) or your favorite topping.

Can also be served with sliced strawberries and whipped cream

Peanut Butter Pancakes

2 eggs

1¾ cups milk

¼ cup vegetable oil

½ cup peanut butter

1¼ cups all-purpose flour

2 tablespoons sugar

2 teaspoons baking powder

1 teaspoon baking soda

1. Heat griddle to 400 degrees (medium high heat)
2. In a large bowl combine eggs, milk, oil, peanut butter
3. Add flour, sugar, baking powder and baking soda and mix until just combined
4. Pour batter about ¼ cup at a time
5. Cook until edges dry and bubbles form
6. Flip cake and finish cooking, about 15 to 30 seconds

Serve with Caramel Sauce (page 54), or Chocolate Sauce (page 53) or your favorite topping

Chai Pancakes

2 eggs

2 cups strong Chai tea

¼ cup vegetable oil

1¾ cups all-purpose flour

2 tablespoons dark brown sugar

2 teaspoons baking powder

1 teaspoon baking soda

1. Heat Griddle to 400 degrees (medium high heat)
2. In a large bowl combine eggs, tea, and oil
3. Add flour, sugar, baking powder and baking soda and mix, until just combined
4. Pour batter about ¼ cup at a time
5. Cook until edges dry and bubbles form
6. Flip cake and finish cooking, about 15 to 30 seconds

Serve with Honey Syrup (page 55), or your favorite topping

Espresso and Cinnamon Pancakes with Caramel Sauce

2 eggs

1 cup milk

¾ cup espresso

¼ teaspoon cinnamon

¼ cup vegetable oil

1¾ cups all-purpose flour

2 tablespoons dark brown sugar

2 teaspoons baking powder

1 teaspoon baking soda

1. Heat griddle to 400 degrees (medium high heat)
2. In a large bowl combine eggs, milk, espresso, cinnamon and oil
3. Add flour, sugar, baking powder and baking soda and mix until just combined
4. Pour batter about ¼ cup at a time
5. Cook until edges dry and bubbles form
6. Flip cake and finish cooking, about 15 to 30 seconds

Top with Caramel Sauce (page 54)

Parisian Pancakes (Cognac & Kahlua)

2 eggs

1¼ cups milk

½ cup espresso

½ oz Cognac

½ oz Kahlua

¼ cup vegetable oil

1¾ cups all-purpose flour

2 tablespoons dark brown sugar

2 teaspoons baking powder

1 teaspoon baking soda

1. Heat griddle to 400 degrees (medium high heat)
2. In a large bowl combine eggs, milk, espresso, cognac, kalhlua and oil
3. Add flour, sugar, baking powder and baking soda and mix until just combined
4. Pour batter about ¼ cup at a time
5. Cook until edges dry and bubbles form
6. Flip cake and finish cooking, about 15 to 30 seconds

Serve with Caramel Sauce (page 54), or Chocolate Sauce (page 53) or your favorite topping

Maple Almond Pancakes

2 eggs

2 cups milk

¼ cup vegetable oil

1 oz Amaretto

1/3 cup maple Syrup

1¾ cups all-purpose flour

2 teaspoons baking powder

1 teaspoon baking soda

½ cup slivered almonds

1. Heat Griddle to 400 degrees (medium high heat)
2. In a large bowl combine eggs, milk, oil, Amaretto, and syrup
3. Add flour, sugar, baking powder and baking soda and mix, until just combined
4. Add almonds
5. Pour batter about ¼ cup at a time
6. Cook until edges dry and bubbles form
7. Flip cake and finish cooking, about 15 to 30 seconds

Honey Almond

2 eggs

2 cups milk

¼ cup vegetable oil

1/3 cup honey

1oz Drambuie

1¾ cups all-purpose flour

2 teaspoons baking powder

1 teaspoon baking soda

¼ cup slivered almonds

1. Heat Griddle to 400 degrees (medium high heat)
2. In a large bowl combine eggs, milk, honey, Drambuie and oil
3. Add flour, sugar, baking powder and baking soda and mix until just combined
4. Add almonds
5. Pour batter about ¼ cup at a time
6. Cook until edges dry and bubbles form
7. Flip cake and finish cooking, about 15 to 30 seconds

Serve with Honey Syrup (page 55), or your favorite topping

Extra Easy Mix-ins

Pancake Mix

8 cups flour

½ cup sugar

1/3 cup baking powder

1/8 cup baking soda

1. Combine all ingredients in mixing bowl and mix for about one minute
2. Store in airtight container

Add-in Pancakes

These add-in recipes can be prepared with our pancake mix recipe (page 49) our basic pancake recipe (page 7) or your favorite brand of pancake mix.

2 cups pancake mix (page 49)

2 cups milk

2 eggs

1 tablespoon oil

½ cup of your favorite add in

1. Add pancake mix to a mixing bowl and using a large spoon create a well in the center

2. Add remaining ingredients to well and mix well

3. Add your "add-in"

4. Pour batter about ¼ cup at a time

5. Cook until edges dry and bubbles form

6. Flip cake and finish cooking, about 15 to 30 seconds

Use the pancake mix recipe on page 49 or your favorite brand of pancake mix to create these easy breakfast treats. Simply add these ingredients to the finished batter.

Almond Pancakes: ½ cup silvered almonds and 1/8 cup almond paste

Apricot Pancakes: ½ cup dried apricots

Blueberry Pancakes: Add ½ cup fresh or frozen blueberries

Blackberry Pancakes: ½ cup fresh blackberries

Butterscotch Crunch Pancakes: ½ cup butterscotch chips and ½ cup granola

Caramel Toffee Crunch Pancakes: Add ½ cup toffee chips and ½ cup granola

Chocolate Chip Pancakes: ½ cup chocolate chips

Favorite Berry Pancakes: Choose your favorite berry or berry combination and add ½ cup to the finished batter.

Peaches & Cream Pancakes: Add ½ cup of diced cooked peaches and ¼ cup half and half or heavy cream. For extra flavor you can also add 1 oz of Southern Comfort or Peach Schnapps

Pecan Pancakes: ½ cup chopped pecans

Spiced Cider Pancakes: Substitute spiced apple cider for milk

Toppings and Fillings

Sweet Cream Sauce

1 cup whipping cream

1 cup (packed) dark brown sugar

1/2 cup sweetened condensed milk

1 teaspoon vanilla

1. Combine cream and brown sugar in medium saucepan stirring over medium heat until sugar is dissolved

2. Bring to a low boil and simmer for five minutes

3. Add condensed milk and vanilla

Chocolate Syrup

3 oz chocolate chips

1 cup sugar

½ cup water

1) Combine water and sugar in a medium saucepan and bring to a boil

2) Keep at boiling for 5 minutes

3) Remove from heat and add chocolate, stir until chocolate is melted

Caramel Sauce

½ cup sugar

3 tablespoons butter

¼ cup heavy cream

1. In medium saucepan heat sugar until melted and color changes to amber
2. Remove from heat and add butter and stir vigorously
3. Mix in heavy cream
4. Serve warm

Honey Syrup

1 cup granulated sugar
2 cups honey
1 cup green tea
1/8 cup fresh lemon juice

1. Combine all ingredients except lemon juice in a large saucepan

2. Bring to a boil

3. Simmer for 10 minutes

4. Remove from heat and add lemon juice

5. Serve warm

Cheese filling

1 pound ricotta cheese

1 (4-ounce) package cream cheese, softened

3 egg yolks (pasteurized)

1/4 cup sugar

1/4 teaspoon salt

1. combine all ingredients and mix well

2. Serve with Blintzes or Crepes

Index

Lightning Source UK Ltd.
Milton Keynes UK
UKOW050908120212

187155UK00001B/60/A

9 780615 156521